Whose Baby Am I?

by

SHIRLEY GREENWAY

photographs by

OXFORD SCIENTIFIC FILMS

Ideals Children's Books   Nashville, Tennessee

Text copyright © 1992 by Shirley Greenway
Photographs copyright © 1992 by Oxford Scientific Films
Ltd. and individual copyright holders

Published by Ideals Publishing Corporation
Nashville, Tennessee 37214

Printed and bound in the United States of America.

Created and designed by Treld Bicknell.

Library of Congress Cataloging-in-Publication Data

Greenway, Shirley.
Whose baby am I?/by Shirley Greenway; photographs
by Oxford Scientific Films.
p.   cm.
Summary: The reader is asked to guess who is the parent
for each of twelve baby animals, and pictures of the
parents include brief information about each species.
ISBN 0-8249-8575-3 (lib. bdg.)
ISBN 0-8249-8562-1 (trade pbk.)
1. Animals—Infancy—Juvenile literature. 2. Animals—
Infancy—Miscellanea—Juvenile literature. [1. Animals—
Infancy. 2. Animals—Miscellanea.] I. Oxford Scientific
Films. II. Title. III. Series
QL763.G74   1992
591.3'9—dc20   92-6133
                                                                     CIP
                                                                      AC

Acknowledgments:
The author and publisher wish to thank the following for permission to reproduce copyright material: **Oxford Scientific Films** for front cover (Tom Ulrich); title page and p. 7 (Leonard Lee Rue III); p. 3 (Kim Westerskov); pp. 4 and 5 (Photo Researchers Inc.–Dan Guravich); p. 6 (Animals Animals–Marcia W. Griffen); p. 8 (Scott Camazine); pp. 10-11 (Stan Osolinski); p. 12 (Philippe Henry); p. 13 (Konrad Wothe); pp. 14 and 15 (Lon E. Lauber); p. 16 (Tony Martin): p. 17 (Mark Hamblin); pp. 18 and 19 (AA–David C. Fritts); pp. 20-21 (Owen Newman); p. 22 (AA–Breck P. Kent); p. 23 (Jack Dermid); p. 24 (Kathie Atkinson); p. 25 and back cover (AA—Dr. E. R. Degginger); p. 26 (Tom Leach); and pp. 28-29 (Malcolm Coe).

Q. We are cygnets.
Whose babies are we?

A. The fluffy, silvery cygnets (SIG · nitz) swim screnely along with their mother—a lovely black swan.

Q. I am a cub.
Whose baby am I?

A. When her cubs are born in the winter, the polar bear cares for them in a cozy den under the Arctic snow. In the spring they tumble out to explore the new world, staying close to their mother.

I am a fawn.

Whose baby am I?

A. A white-tailed doe often hides her newborn fawn in the long grasses. Once she knows that he is safe, the doe licks him clean and helps him to stand on his own.

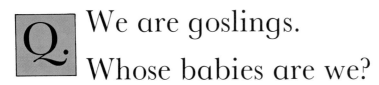 We are goslings.

Whose babies are we?

A. This Canada goose has gathered a whole fleet of goslings around her. Some of the little ones are her own babies, others she has taken along for a swimming lesson.

Q. I am a kitten.

Whose baby am I?

A. This kitten, with its soft, spotted fur, is a lynx (lingks). He is one of the big cats and will become a sharp-eyed hunter, just like his mother.

Q. I am an eaglet.
Whose baby am I?

A. This gangly, gray ball of fluff will look very different when she grows up. She will become a strong, broad-winged bird of prey like her parent—a magnificent bald eagle.

I am a pup.

Whose baby am I?

 This sad-eyed, young seal pup waits on the rocky shore for his mother, a gray seal. She hunts for fish in the sea, but her pup is not yet fat enough to stay warm in the cold water.

We are lambs.

Whose babies are we?

A. Shaggy, white Dall (doll) sheep graze in high mountain meadows in the summer. When the ewes (yooz) and their lambs gather for an afternoon rest, the youngest finds the most comfortable spot.

I am a mouse.

Whose baby am I?

 The plump little dormouse comes out to feed at night. She builds a doorless, round nest where she raises her young in summer and sleeps the cold winters away.

Q. I am a tadpole.
Whose baby am I?

A. Tadpoles are baby frogs. They hatch in the water from tiny, black eggs. They grow legs, lose their gills and tails, and soon become frogs—at home on land or in water.

I am a joey.
Whose baby am I?

 A. The joey peeking from her mother's warm pouch is an Australian red-necked wallaby. She is a marsupial (mar · SOO · pee · uhl) mammal, and for many weeks she has been growing inside the pouch. Then out she pops to look and learn and feed on grass.

Q. I am a foal.

Whose baby am I?

The foal's mother is a zebra, with the same crisp brown stripes and knobby knees. They live with the herd, roaming the African plains.

Baby animals sometimes have special names:

 The swan has cygnets.

 The goose has goslings.

 The polar bear has cubs.

 The lynx has a kitten.

 The doe has a fawn.

 The eagle has eaglets.

 The seal has a pup.

 The frog has eggs and tadpoles.

 The sheep has lambs.

 The wallaby has a joey.

 The dormouse has baby mice.

 The zebra has a foal.

Index